THE **GRATITUDE** JOURNAL

365 DAYS OF **GRATITUDE**

Created by Eric & Kelly Dykstra

#The**Gratitude**Project
The**Gratitude**Project.tv

The **Gratitude** Journal

365 days of **Gratitude**

Created by Eric & Kelly Dykstra

#The**Gratitude**Project
The**Gratitude**Project.tv

CROSSING CHURCH
PUBLISHING
freegrace.tv
Guilt free. Grace full.

Created by Eric & Kelly Dykstra

Published by Crossing Church Publishing
829 School Street, Elk River, Minnesota 55330

www.freegrace.tv

First Printing: 2015

ISBN 978-0-9896828-3-1

Gratitude makes life better! Studies show that the more grateful we are, the better our relationships, the higher our incomes, and the healthier we live.

The **Gratitude** Project is an initiative to cause us to develop a habit of gratefulness, no matter our circumstances. This will change our attitudes and cause us to be happier, healthier people.

David says in the Scriptures:
Praise the Lord, O my soul, and forget not all His benefits! (Psalms 103:2)

We need to remember all the good things God is doing for us. Don't forget to be grateful!

The Apostle Paul in the Scriptures says:
Give thanks in all circumstances; for this God's will for you in Christ Jesus. (1 Thessalonians 5:18)

God's desire for us is to be grateful at all times, no matter our circumstances. This will cause us to live more successful lives in the flow of God's grace and plan for us!

*The **Gratitude** Journal* you are holding in your hands is a simple tool you can use to develop the habit of gratefulness.

Every day, no matter what is going on in your life, list five specific things you can be grateful for. Listing five specific things (instead of just two or three) causes you to search beyond the basics of food, clothing, shelter, and family--and actually *notice* other good things that God is actively doing in your life to bless you every day.

A good parking spot; the A on your child's homework; a decrease in the price of gas or an increase in your savings account. All of these kinds of things are God's hand at work in your life! Taking the time to notice them will cause you to be favor-minded and to live with your eyes on God instead of the negative things in your life.

Our hope and prayer is that *The **Gratitude** Journal* changes your thinking, which will change your attitude and, ultimately, change your life. God is blessing you! We hope this helps you see it and brings you great joy!

Eric & Kelly

I am **grateful** for...

Date ______________

1. ____
____

2. ____
____

3. ____
____

4. ____
____

5. ____
____

Date ______________

1. ____
____

2. ____
____

3. ____
____

4. ____
____

5. ____
____

I am **grateful** for...

Date ______________

1. ____
____

2. ____
____

3. ____
____

4. ____
____

5. ____
____

Date ______________

1. ____
____

2. ____
____

3. ____
____

4. ____
____

5. ____
____

I am **grateful** for...

Date 1/9/21

1. I am grateful to spend time with and to hug Brooklyn & Ben
2. I am grateful for Jenna to come out & help & show love to the children.
3. I am grateful for the time we can spend playing games together. PARKS!
4. I am grateful for snow and sledding!
5. I am grateful my grandchildren love to be outside in God's creation

Date 1/10/21

1. I am grateful for friends to fish with.
2. I am grateful for winter & ice fishing
3. I am grateful we have an gear & clothing for fishing in winter.
4. I am grateful for Dave who organizes & makes sure I have what I need for adventures
5. I am grateful to be able to go to church and worship.

I am **grateful** for...

Date 1/11/21

1. I am grateful to be able to work my own schedule @ work

2. I am grateful Derek and his involvement in Tri-State

3. I am grateful for Cody working at Tri-State.

4. I am grateful for Lauren reaching out for help in her marriage

5. I am grateful for all my grandchildren.

Date ____________

1.

2.

3.

4.

5.

I am **grateful** for...

Date 1/13/21

1. I am grateful for my time with Bri today

2. I am grateful for the opportunity to go for a flight in our plane

3. I am grateful for the option to go on a vacation next week

4. I am grateful for Betsy loving me and being excited to see me.

5. I am grateful for sleep AND rest for my body.

Date

1.

2.

3.

4.

5.

I am **grateful** for...

Date ______________

1. ____
____

2. ____
____

3. ____
____

4. ____
____

5. ____
____

Date ______________

1. ____
____

2. ____
____

3. ____
____

4. ____
____

5. ____
____

I am **grateful** for...

Date ______________

1. ____
____

2. ____
____

3. ____
____

4. ____
____

5. ____
____

Date ______________

1. ____
____

2. ____
____

3. ____
____

4. ____
____

5. ____
____

I am **grateful** for...

Date _______________

1. ____
____

2. ____
____

3. ____
____

4. ____
____

5. ____
____

Date _______________

1. ____
____

2. ____
____

3. ____
____

4. ____
____

5. ____
____

I am **grateful** for...

Date ______________

1. ____
____

2. ____
____

3. ____
____

4. ____
____

5. ____
____

Date ______________

1. ____
____

2. ____
____

3. ____
____

4. ____
____

5. ____
____

I am **grateful** for...

Date ______________

1. ____
____

2. ____
____

3. ____
____

4. ____
____

5. ____
____

Date ______________

1. ____
____

2. ____
____

3. ____
____

4. ____
____

5. ____
____

I am **grateful** for...

Date ______________

1. ____
____

2. ____
____

3. ____
____

4. ____
____

5. ____
____

Date ______________

1. ____
____

2. ____
____

3. ____
____

4. ____
____

5. ____
____

I am **grateful** for...

Date ______________

1. ____
____

2. ____
____

3. ____
____

4. ____
____

5. ____
____

Date ______________

1. ____
____

2. ____
____

3. ____
____

4. ____
____

5. ____
____

I am **grateful** for...

Date _______________

1. ____

____

2. ____

____

3. ____

____

4. ____

____

5. ____

____

Date _______________

1. ____

____

2. ____

____

3. ____

____

4. ____

____

5. ____

____

I am **grateful** for...

Date ______________

1. ____
____

2. ____
____

3. ____
____

4. ____
____

5. ____
____

Date ______________

1. ____
____

2. ____
____

3. ____
____

4. ____
____

5. ____
____

I am **grateful** for...

Date ______________

1. ____
____

2. ____
____

3. ____
____

4. ____
____

5. ____
____

Date ______________

1. ____
____

2. ____
____

3. ____
____

4. ____
____

5. ____
____

I am **grateful** for...

Date _______________

1. ____
____

2. ____
____

3. ____
____

4. ____
____

5. ____
____

Date _______________

1. ____
____

2. ____
____

3. ____
____

4. ____
____

5. ____
____

I am **grateful** for...

Date ______________

1. ____
____

2. ____
____

3. ____
____

4. ____
____

5. ____
____

Date ______________

1. ____
____

2. ____
____

3. ____
____

4. ____
____

5. ____
____

I am **grateful** for...

Date _______________

1. ____
____

2. ____
____

3. ____
____

4. ____
____

5. ____
____

Date _______________

1. ____
____

2. ____
____

3. ____
____

4. ____
____

5. ____
____

I am **grateful** for...

Date ______________

1. ____
____

2. ____
____

3. ____
____

4. ____
____

5. ____
____

Date ______________

1. ____
____

2. ____
____

3. ____
____

4. ____
____

5. ____
____

I am **grateful** for...

Date ______________

1. ____
____

2. ____
____

3. ____
____

4. ____
____

5. ____
____

Date ______________

1. ____
____

2. ____
____

3. ____
____

4. ____
____

5. ____
____

I am **grateful** for...

Date ______________

1. ____
____

2. ____
____

3. ____
____

4. ____
____

5. ____
____

Date ______________

1. ____
____

2. ____
____

3. ____
____

4. ____
____

5. ____
____

I am **grateful** for...

Date ______________

1. ____
____

2. ____
____

3. ____
____

4. ____
____

5. ____
____

Date ______________

1. ____
____

2. ____
____

3. ____
____

4. ____
____

5. ____
____

I am **grateful** for...

Date ______________

1. ____
____

2. ____
____

3. ____
____

4. ____
____

5. ____
____

Date ______________

1. ____
____

2. ____
____

3. ____
____

4. ____
____

5. ____
____

I am **grateful** for...

Date _______________

1. ____
____

2. ____
____

3. ____
____

4. ____
____

5. ____
____

Date _______________

1. ____
____

2. ____
____

3. ____
____

4. ____
____

5. ____
____

I am **grateful** for...

Date ______________

1. ____
____

2. ____
____

3. ____
____

4. ____
____

5. ____
____

Date ______________

1. ____
____

2. ____
____

3. ____
____

4. ____
____

5. ____
____

I am **grateful** for...

Date ______________

1. ____

____

2. ____

____

3. ____

____

4. ____

____

5. ____

____

Date ______________

1. ____

____

2. ____

____

3. ____

____

4. ____

____

5. ____

____

I am **grateful** for...

Date _______________

1. ____
____

2. ____
____

3. ____
____

4. ____
____

5. ____
____

Date _______________

1. ____
____

2. ____
____

3. ____
____

4. ____
____

5. ____
____

I am **grateful** for...

Date ______________

1. ____
____

2. ____
____

3. ____
____

4. ____
____

5. ____
____

Date ______________

1. ____
____

2. ____
____

3. ____
____

4. ____
____

5. ____
____

I am **grateful** for...

Date ______________

1. ____
____

2. ____
____

3. ____
____

4. ____
____

5. ____
____

Date ______________

1. ____
____

2. ____
____

3. ____
____

4. ____
____

5. ____
____

I am **grateful** for...

Date ______________

1. ____
____

2. ____
____

3. ____
____

4. ____
____

5. ____
____

Date ______________

1. ____
____

2. ____
____

3. ____
____

4. ____
____

5. ____
____

I am **grateful** for...

Date ______________

1. ____
____

2. ____
____

3. ____
____

4. ____
____

5. ____
____

Date ______________

1. ____
____

2. ____
____

3. ____
____

4. ____
____

5. ____
____

I am **grateful** for...

Date ______________

1. ____
____

2. ____
____

3. ____
____

4. ____
____

5. ____
____

Date ______________

1. ____
____

2. ____
____

3. ____
____

4. ____
____

5. ____
____

I am **grateful** for...

Date ______________

1. ____
____

2. ____
____

3. ____
____

4. ____
____

5. ____
____

Date ______________

1. ____
____

2. ____
____

3. ____
____

4. ____
____

5. ____
____

I am **grateful** for...

Date ______________

1. ____
____

2. ____
____

3. ____
____

4. ____
____

5. ____
____

Date ______________

1. ____
____

2. ____
____

3. ____
____

4. ____
____

5. ____
____

I am **grateful** for...

Date _______________

1. ____
____

2. ____
____

3. ____
____

4. ____
____

5. ____
____

Date _______________

1. ____
____

2. ____
____

3. ____
____

4. ____
____

5. ____
____

I am **grateful** for...

Date _______________

1. ____
____

2. ____
____

3. ____
____

4. ____
____

5. ____
____

Date _______________

1. ____
____

2. ____
____

3. ____
____

4. ____
____

5. ____
____

I am **grateful** for...

Date _______________

1. ____
____

2. ____
____

3. ____
____

4. ____
____

5. ____
____

Date _______________

1. ____
____

2. ____
____

3. ____
____

4. ____
____

5. ____
____

I am **grateful** for...

Date _______________

1. ____
____

2. ____
____

3. ____
____

4. ____
____

5. ____
____

Date _______________

1. ____
____

2. ____
____

3. ____
____

4. ____
____

5. ____
____

I am **grateful** for...

Date _______________

1. ____
____

2. ____
____

3. ____
____

4. ____
____

5. ____
____

Date _______________

1. ____
____

2. ____
____

3. ____
____

4. ____
____

5. ____
____

I am **grateful** for...

Date ______________

1. ____
____

2. ____
____

3. ____
____

4. ____
____

5. ____
____

Date ______________

1. ____
____

2. ____
____

3. ____
____

4. ____
____

5. ____
____

I am **grateful** for...

Date ______________

1. ____
____

2. ____
____

3. ____
____

4. ____
____

5. ____
____

Date ______________

1. ____
____

2. ____
____

3. ____
____

4. ____
____

5. ____
____

I am **grateful** for...

Date ______________

1. ____
____

2. ____
____

3. ____
____

4. ____
____

5. ____
____

Date ______________

1. ____
____

2. ____
____

3. ____
____

4. ____
____

5. ____
____

I am **grateful** for...

Date ______________

1. ____
____

2. ____
____

3. ____
____

4. ____
____

5. ____
____

Date ______________

1. ____
____

2. ____
____

3. ____
____

4. ____
____

5. ____
____

I am **grateful** for...

Date _______________

1. ____
____

2. ____
____

3. ____
____

4. ____
____

5. ____
____

Date _______________

1. ____
____

2. ____
____

3. ____
____

4. ____
____

5. ____
____

I am **grateful** for...

Date ______________

1. ____
____

2. ____
____

3. ____
____

4. ____
____

5. ____
____

Date ______________

1. ____
____

2. ____
____

3. ____
____

4. ____
____

5. ____
____

I am **grateful** for...

Date _______________

1. ____
____

2. ____
____

3. ____
____

4. ____
____

5. ____
____

Date _______________

1. ____
____

2. ____
____

3. ____
____

4. ____
____

5. ____
____

I am **grateful** for...

Date ______________

1. ____
____

2. ____
____

3. ____
____

4. ____
____

5. ____
____

Date ______________

1. ____
____

2. ____
____

3. ____
____

4. ____
____

5. ____
____

I am **grateful** for...

Date ______________

1. ____
____

2. ____
____

3. ____
____

4. ____
____

5. ____
____

Date ______________

1. ____
____

2. ____
____

3. ____
____

4. ____
____

5. ____
____

I am **grateful** for...

Date _______________

1. ____
____

2. ____
____

3. ____
____

4. ____
____

5. ____
____

Date _______________

1. ____
____

2. ____
____

3. ____
____

4. ____
____

5. ____
____

I am **grateful** for...

Date _______________

1. ____
____

2. ____
____

3. ____
____

4. ____
____

5. ____
____

Date _______________

1. ____
____

2. ____
____

3. ____
____

4. ____
____

5. ____
____

I am **grateful** for...

Date ______________

1. ____

____

2. ____

____

3. ____

____

4. ____

____

5. ____

____

Date ______________

1. ____

____

2. ____

____

3. ____

____

4. ____

____

5. ____

____

I am **grateful** for...

Date ______________

1. ____
____

2. ____
____

3. ____
____

4. ____
____

5. ____
____

Date ______________

1. ____
____

2. ____
____

3. ____
____

4. ____
____

5. ____
____

I am **grateful** for...

Date ______________

1. ____
____

2. ____
____

3. ____
____

4. ____
____

5. ____
____

Date ______________

1. ____
____

2. ____
____

3. ____
____

4. ____
____

5. ____
____

I am **grateful** for...

Date ______________

1. ____
____

2. ____
____

3. ____
____

4. ____
____

5. ____
____

Date ______________

1. ____
____

2. ____
____

3. ____
____

4. ____
____

5. ____
____

I am **grateful** for...

Date ______________

1. ____
____

2. ____
____

3. ____
____

4. ____
____

5. ____
____

Date ______________

1. ____
____

2. ____
____

3. ____
____

4. ____
____

5. ____
____

I am **grateful** for...

Date ______________

1. ____
____

2. ____
____

3. ____
____

4. ____
____

5. ____
____

Date ______________

1. ____
____

2. ____
____

3. ____
____

4. ____
____

5. ____
____

I am **grateful** for...

Date ______________

1. ____
____

2. ____
____

3. ____
____

4. ____
____

5. ____
____

Date ______________

1. ____
____

2. ____
____

3. ____
____

4. ____
____

5. ____
____

I am **grateful** for...

Date ______________

1. ____
____

2. ____
____

3. ____
____

4. ____
____

5. ____
____

Date ______________

1. ____
____

2. ____
____

3. ____
____

4. ____
____

5. ____
____

I am **grateful** for...

Date _______________

1. ____
____

2. ____
____

3. ____
____

4. ____
____

5. ____
____

Date _______________

1. ____
____

2. ____
____

3. ____
____

4. ____
____

5. ____
____

I am **grateful** for...

Date ______________

1. ____

____

2. ____

____

3. ____

____

4. ____

____

5. ____

____

Date ______________

1. ____

____

2. ____

____

3. ____

____

4. ____

____

5. ____

____

I am **grateful** for...

Date ______________

1. ____
____

2. ____
____

3. ____
____

4. ____
____

5. ____
____

Date ______________

1. ____
____

2. ____
____

3. ____
____

4. ____
____

5. ____
____

I am **grateful** for...

Date ______________

1. ____
____

2. ____
____

3. ____
____

4. ____
____

5. ____
____

Date ______________

1. ____
____

2. ____
____

3. ____
____

4. ____
____

5. ____
____

I am **grateful** for...

Date ______________

1. ____
____

2. ____
____

3. ____
____

4. ____
____

5. ____
____

Date ______________

1. ____
____

2. ____
____

3. ____
____

4. ____
____

5. ____
____

I am **grateful** for...

Date ______________

1. ____
____

2. ____
____

3. ____
____

4. ____
____

5. ____
____

Date ______________

1. ____
____

2. ____
____

3. ____
____

4. ____
____

5. ____
____

I am **grateful** for...

Date ______________

1. ____
____

2. ____
____

3. ____
____

4. ____
____

5. ____
____

Date ______________

1. ____
____

2. ____
____

3. ____
____

4. ____
____

5. ____
____

I am **grateful** for...

Date ______________

1. ____
____

2. ____
____

3. ____
____

4. ____
____

5. ____
____

Date ______________

1. ____
____

2. ____
____

3. ____
____

4. ____
____

5. ____
____

I am **grateful** for...

Date ______________

1. ____
____

2. ____
____

3. ____
____

4. ____
____

5. ____
____

Date ______________

1. ____
____

2. ____
____

3. ____
____

4. ____
____

5. ____
____

I am **grateful** for...

Date _______________

1. ____
____

2. ____
____

3. ____
____

4. ____
____

5. ____
____

Date _______________

1. ____
____

2. ____
____

3. ____
____

4. ____
____

5. ____
____

I am **grateful** for...

Date ______________

1. ____
____

2. ____
____

3. ____
____

4. ____
____

5. ____
____

Date ______________

1. ____
____

2. ____
____

3. ____
____

4. ____
____

5. ____
____

I am **grateful** for...

Date ______________

1. ____
____

2. ____
____

3. ____
____

4. ____
____

5. ____
____

Date ______________

1. ____
____

2. ____
____

3. ____
____

4. ____
____

5. ____
____

I am **grateful** for...

Date ______________

1. ____
____

2. ____
____

3. ____
____

4. ____
____

5. ____
____

Date ______________

1. ____
____

2. ____
____

3. ____
____

4. ____
____

5. ____
____

I am **grateful** for...

Date ______________

1. ____
____

2. ____
____

3. ____
____

4. ____
____

5. ____
____

Date ______________

1. ____
____

2. ____
____

3. ____
____

4. ____
____

5. ____
____

I am **grateful** for...

Date _______________

1. ____
____

2. ____
____

3. ____
____

4. ____
____

5. ____
____

Date _______________

1. ____
____

2. ____
____

3. ____
____

4. ____
____

5. ____
____

I am **grateful** for...

Date ______________

1. ____
____

2. ____
____

3. ____
____

4. ____
____

5. ____
____

Date ______________

1. ____
____

2. ____
____

3. ____
____

4. ____
____

5. ____
____

I am **grateful** for...

Date _______________

1. ____
____

2. ____
____

3. ____
____

4. ____
____

5. ____
____

Date _______________

1. ____
____

2. ____
____

3. ____
____

4. ____
____

5. ____
____

I am **grateful** for...

Date ______________

1. ____
____

2. ____
____

3. ____
____

4. ____
____

5. ____
____

Date ______________

1. ____
____

2. ____
____

3. ____
____

4. ____
____

5. ____
____

I am **grateful** for...

Date ______________

1. ____
____

2. ____
____

3. ____
____

4. ____
____

5. ____
____

Date ______________

1. ____
____

2. ____
____

3. ____
____

4. ____
____

5. ____
____

I am **grateful** for...

Date ______________

1. ____
____

2. ____
____

3. ____
____

4. ____
____

5. ____
____

Date ______________

1. ____
____

2. ____
____

3. ____
____

4. ____
____

5. ____
____

I am **grateful** for...

Date _______________

1. ____
____

2. ____
____

3. ____
____

4. ____
____

5. ____
____

Date _______________

1. ____
____

2. ____
____

3. ____
____

4. ____
____

5. ____
____

I am **grateful** for...

Date ______________

1. ____
____

2. ____
____

3. ____
____

4. ____
____

5. ____
____

Date ______________

1. ____
____

2. ____
____

3. ____
____

4. ____
____

5. ____
____

I am **grateful** for...

Date ______________

1. ____

____

2. ____

____

3. ____

____

4. ____

____

5. ____

____

Date ______________

1. ____

____

2. ____

____

3. ____

____

4. ____

____

5. ____

____

I am **grateful** for...

Date ______________

1. ____
____

2. ____
____

3. ____
____

4. ____
____

5. ____
____

Date ______________

1. ____
____

2. ____
____

3. ____
____

4. ____
____

5. ____
____

I am **grateful** for...

Date _______________

1. ____
____

2. ____
____

3. ____
____

4. ____
____

5. ____
____

Date _______________

1. ____
____

2. ____
____

3. ____
____

4. ____
____

5. ____
____

I am **grateful** for...

Date ______________

1. ____
____

2. ____
____

3. ____
____

4. ____
____

5. ____
____

Date ______________

1. ____
____

2. ____
____

3. ____
____

4. ____
____

5. ____
____

I am **grateful** for...

Date _______________

1. ____
____

2. ____
____

3. ____
____

4. ____
____

5. ____
____

Date _______________

1. ____
____

2. ____
____

3. ____
____

4. ____
____

5. ____
____

I am **grateful** for...

Date ______________

1. ____
____

2. ____
____

3. ____
____

4. ____
____

5. ____
____

Date ______________

1. ____
____

2. ____
____

3. ____
____

4. ____
____

5. ____
____

I am **grateful** for...

Date _______________

1. ____
____

2. ____
____

3. ____
____

4. ____
____

5. ____
____

Date _______________

1. ____
____

2. ____
____

3. ____
____

4. ____
____

5. ____
____

I am **grateful** for...

Date ______________

1. ____
____

2. ____
____

3. ____
____

4. ____
____

5. ____
____

Date ______________

1. ____
____

2. ____
____

3. ____
____

4. ____
____

5. ____
____

I am **grateful** for...

Date _______________

1. ____

____

2. ____

____

3. ____

____

4. ____

____

5. ____

____

Date _______________

1. ____

____

2. ____

____

3. ____

____

4. ____

____

5. ____

____

I am **grateful** for...

Date ______________

1. ____
____

2. ____
____

3. ____
____

4. ____
____

5. ____
____

Date ______________

1. ____
____

2. ____
____

3. ____
____

4. ____
____

5. ____
____

I am **grateful** for...

Date _______________

1. ____
____

2. ____
____

3. ____
____

4. ____
____

5. ____
____

Date _______________

1. ____
____

2. ____
____

3. ____
____

4. ____
____

5. ____
____

I am **grateful** for...

Date ______________

1. ____
____

2. ____
____

3. ____
____

4. ____
____

5. ____
____

Date ______________

1. ____
____

2. ____
____

3. ____
____

4. ____
____

5. ____
____

I am **grateful** for...

Date ______________

1. ____
____

2. ____
____

3. ____
____

4. ____
____

5. ____
____

Date ______________

1. ____
____

2. ____
____

3. ____
____

4. ____
____

5. ____
____

I am **grateful** for...

Date ______________

1. ____

____

2. ____

____

3. ____

____

4. ____

____

5. ____

____

Date ______________

1. ____

____

2. ____

____

3. ____

____

4. ____

____

5. ____

____

I am **grateful** for...

Date ______________

1. ____
____

2. ____
____

3. ____
____

4. ____
____

5. ____
____

Date ______________

1. ____
____

2. ____
____

3. ____
____

4. ____
____

5. ____
____

I am **grateful** for...

Date ______________

1. ____
____

2. ____
____

3. ____
____

4. ____
____

5. ____
____

Date ______________

1. ____
____

2. ____
____

3. ____
____

4. ____
____

5. ____
____

I am **grateful** for...

Date ______________

1. ____
____

2. ____
____

3. ____
____

4. ____
____

5. ____
____

Date ______________

1. ____
____

2. ____
____

3. ____
____

4. ____
____

5. ____
____

I am **grateful** for...

Date ______________

1. ____

____

2. ____

____

3. ____

____

4. ____

____

5. ____

____

Date ______________

1. ____

____

2. ____

____

3. ____

____

4. ____

____

5. ____

____

I am **grateful** for...

Date _______________

1. ____
____

2. ____
____

3. ____
____

4. ____
____

5. ____
____

Date _______________

1. ____
____

2. ____
____

3. ____
____

4. ____
____

5. ____
____

I am **grateful** for...

Date ______________

1. ____
____

2. ____
____

3. ____
____

4. ____
____

5. ____
____

Date ______________

1. ____
____

2. ____
____

3. ____
____

4. ____
____

5. ____
____

I am **grateful** for...

Date ______________

1. ____
____

2. ____
____

3. ____
____

4. ____
____

5. ____
____

Date ______________

1. ____
____

2. ____
____

3. ____
____

4. ____
____

5. ____
____

I am **grateful** for...

Date ______________

1. ____
____

2. ____
____

3. ____
____

4. ____
____

5. ____
____

Date ______________

1. ____
____

2. ____
____

3. ____
____

4. ____
____

5. ____
____

I am **grateful** for...

Date ______________

1. ____
____

2. ____
____

3. ____
____

4. ____
____

5. ____
____

Date ______________

1. ____
____

2. ____
____

3. ____
____

4. ____
____

5. ____
____

I am **grateful** for…

Date ______________

1. ____
____

2. ____
____

3. ____
____

4. ____
____

5. ____
____

Date ______________

1. ____
____

2. ____
____

3. ____
____

4. ____
____

5. ____
____

I am **grateful** for...

Date _______________

1. ____
____

2. ____
____

3. ____
____

4. ____
____

5. ____
____

Date _______________

1. ____
____

2. ____
____

3. ____
____

4. ____
____

5. ____
____

I am **grateful** for...

Date ______________

1. ____
____

2. ____
____

3. ____
____

4. ____
____

5. ____
____

Date ______________

1. ____
____

2. ____
____

3. ____
____

4. ____
____

5. ____
____

I am **grateful** for...

Date ______________

1. ____
____

2. ____
____

3. ____
____

4. ____
____

5. ____
____

Date ______________

1. ____
____

2. ____
____

3. ____
____

4. ____
____

5. ____
____

I am **grateful** for...

Date ______________

1. ____
____

2. ____
____

3. ____
____

4. ____
____

5. ____
____

Date ______________

1. ____
____

2. ____
____

3. ____
____

4. ____
____

5. ____
____

I am **grateful** for...

Date ______________

1. ____
____

2. ____
____

3. ____
____

4. ____
____

5. ____
____

Date ______________

1. ____
____

2. ____
____

3. ____
____

4. ____
____

5. ____
____

I am **grateful** for...

Date ______________

1. ____

____

2. ____

____

3. ____

____

4. ____

____

5. ____

____

Date ______________

1. ____

____

2. ____

____

3. ____

____

4. ____

____

5. ____

____

I am **grateful** for...

Date ______________

1. ____
____

2. ____
____

3. ____
____

4. ____
____

5. ____
____

Date ______________

1. ____
____

2. ____
____

3. ____
____

4. ____
____

5. ____
____

I am **grateful** for...

Date ______________

1. ____
____

2. ____
____

3. ____
____

4. ____
____

5. ____
____

Date ______________

1. ____
____

2. ____
____

3. ____
____

4. ____
____

5. ____
____

I am **grateful** for...

Date ______________

1. ____
____

2. ____
____

3. ____
____

4. ____
____

5. ____
____

Date ______________

1. ____
____

2. ____
____

3. ____
____

4. ____
____

5. ____
____

I am **grateful** for...

Date ______________

1. ____
____

2. ____
____

3. ____
____

4. ____
____

5. ____
____

Date ______________

1. ____
____

2. ____
____

3. ____
____

4. ____
____

5. ____
____

I am **grateful** for...

Date ______________

1. ____
____

2. ____
____

3. ____
____

4. ____
____

5. ____
____

Date ______________

1. ____
____

2. ____
____

3. ____
____

4. ____
____

5. ____
____

I am **grateful** for...

Date ______________

1. ____
____

2. ____
____

3. ____
____

4. ____
____

5. ____
____

Date ______________

1. ____
____

2. ____
____

3. ____
____

4. ____
____

5. ____
____

I am **grateful** for...

Date _______________

1. ____

____

2. ____

____

3. ____

____

4. ____

____

5. ____

____

Date _______________

1. ____

____

2. ____

____

3. ____

____

4. ____

____

5. ____

____

I am **grateful** for...

Date ______________

1. ____
____

2. ____
____

3. ____
____

4. ____
____

5. ____
____

Date ______________

1. ____
____

2. ____
____

3. ____
____

4. ____
____

5. ____
____

I am **grateful** for...

Date ______________

1. ____
____

2. ____
____

3. ____
____

4. ____
____

5. ____
____

Date ______________

1. ____
____

2. ____
____

3. ____
____

4. ____
____

5. ____
____

I am **grateful** for...

Date _______________

1. ____
____

2. ____
____

3. ____
____

4. ____
____

5. ____
____

Date _______________

1. ____
____

2. ____
____

3. ____
____

4. ____
____

5. ____
____

I am **grateful** for...

Date ______________

1. ____
____

2. ____
____

3. ____
____

4. ____
____

5. ____
____

Date ______________

1. ____
____

2. ____
____

3. ____
____

4. ____
____

5. ____
____

I am **grateful** for...

Date ______________

1. ____
____

2. ____
____

3. ____
____

4. ____
____

5. ____
____

Date ______________

1. ____
____

2. ____
____

3. ____
____

4. ____
____

5. ____
____

I am **grateful** for...

Date ______________

1. ____
____

2. ____
____

3. ____
____

4. ____
____

5. ____
____

Date ______________

1. ____
____

2. ____
____

3. ____
____

4. ____
____

5. ____
____

I am **grateful** for...

Date ______________

1. ____
____

2. ____
____

3. ____
____

4. ____
____

5. ____
____

Date ______________

1. ____
____

2. ____
____

3. ____
____

4. ____
____

5. ____
____

I am **grateful** for...

Date ______________

1. ____
____

2. ____
____

3. ____
____

4. ____
____

5. ____
____

Date ______________

1. ____
____

2. ____
____

3. ____
____

4. ____
____

5. ____
____

I am **grateful** for...

Date ______________

1. ____
____

2. ____
____

3. ____
____

4. ____
____

5. ____
____

Date ______________

1. ____
____

2. ____
____

3. ____
____

4. ____
____

5. ____
____

I am **grateful** for...

Date ______________

1. ____
____

2. ____
____

3. ____
____

4. ____
____

5. ____
____

Date ______________

1. ____
____

2. ____
____

3. ____
____

4. ____
____

5. ____
____

I am **grateful** for...

Date ______________

1. ____
____

2. ____
____

3. ____
____

4. ____
____

5. ____
____

Date ______________

1. ____
____

2. ____
____

3. ____
____

4. ____
____

5. ____
____

I am **grateful** for...

Date ______________

1. ____
____

2. ____
____

3. ____
____

4. ____
____

5. ____
____

Date ______________

1. ____
____

2. ____
____

3. ____
____

4. ____
____

5. ____
____

I am **grateful** for...

Date ______________

1. ____
____

2. ____
____

3. ____
____

4. ____
____

5. ____
____

Date ______________

1. ____
____

2. ____
____

3. ____
____

4. ____
____

5. ____
____

I am **grateful** for...

Date ______________

1. ____
____

2. ____
____

3. ____
____

4. ____
____

5. ____
____

Date ______________

1. ____
____

2. ____
____

3. ____
____

4. ____
____

5. ____
____

I am **grateful** for...

Date ______________

1. ____
____

2. ____
____

3. ____
____

4. ____
____

5. ____
____

Date ______________

1. ____
____

2. ____
____

3. ____
____

4. ____
____

5. ____
____

I am **grateful** for...

Date ______________

1. ____
____

2. ____
____

3. ____
____

4. ____
____

5. ____
____

Date ______________

1. ____
____

2. ____
____

3. ____
____

4. ____
____

5. ____
____

I am **grateful** for...

Date ______________

1. ____
____

2. ____
____

3. ____
____

4. ____
____

5. ____
____

Date ______________

1. ____
____

2. ____
____

3. ____
____

4. ____
____

5. ____
____

I am **grateful** for...

Date _______________

1. ____
____

2. ____
____

3. ____
____

4. ____
____

5. ____
____

Date _______________

1. ____
____

2. ____
____

3. ____
____

4. ____
____

5. ____
____

I am **grateful** for...

Date ______________

1. ____
____

2. ____
____

3. ____
____

4. ____
____

5. ____
____

Date ______________

1. ____
____

2. ____
____

3. ____
____

4. ____
____

5. ____
____

I am **grateful** for...

Date ______________

1. ____
____

2. ____
____

3. ____
____

4. ____
____

5. ____
____

Date ______________

1. ____
____

2. ____
____

3. ____
____

4. ____
____

5. ____
____

I am **grateful** for...

Date ______________

1. ____
____

2. ____
____

3. ____
____

4. ____
____

5. ____
____

Date ______________

1. ____
____

2. ____
____

3. ____
____

4. ____
____

5. ____
____

I am **grateful** for...

Date ________________

1. ____
____

2. ____
____

3. ____
____

4. ____
____

5. ____
____

Date ________________

1. ____
____

2. ____
____

3. ____
____

4. ____
____

5. ____
____

I am **grateful** for...

Date ______________

1. ____
____

2. ____
____

3. ____
____

4. ____
____

5. ____
____

Date ______________

1. ____
____

2. ____
____

3. ____
____

4. ____
____

5. ____
____

I am **grateful** for...

Date _______________

1. ____
____

2. ____
____

3. ____
____

4. ____
____

5. ____
____

Date _______________

1. ____
____

2. ____
____

3. ____
____

4. ____
____

5. ____
____

I am **grateful** for...

Date ______________

1. ____
____

2. ____
____

3. ____
____

4. ____
____

5. ____
____

Date ______________

1. ____
____

2. ____
____

3. ____
____

4. ____
____

5. ____
____

I am **grateful** for...

Date ______________

1. ____
____

2. ____
____

3. ____
____

4. ____
____

5. ____
____

Date ______________

1. ____
____

2. ____
____

3. ____
____

4. ____
____

5. ____
____

I am **grateful** for...

Date _______________

1. ____
____

2. ____
____

3. ____
____

4. ____
____

5. ____
____

Date _______________

1. ____
____

2. ____
____

3. ____
____

4. ____
____

5. ____
____

I am **grateful** for...

Date ______________

1. ____
____

2. ____
____

3. ____
____

4. ____
____

5. ____
____

Date ______________

1. ____
____

2. ____
____

3. ____
____

4. ____
____

5. ____
____

I am **grateful** for...

Date ______________

1. ____
____

2. ____
____

3. ____
____

4. ____
____

5. ____
____

Date ______________

1. ____
____

2. ____
____

3. ____
____

4. ____
____

5. ____
____

I am **grateful** for...

Date ______________

1. ____
____

2. ____
____

3. ____
____

4. ____
____

5. ____
____

Date ______________

1. ____
____

2. ____
____

3. ____
____

4. ____
____

5. ____
____

I am **grateful** for...

Date ______________

1. ____
____

2. ____
____

3. ____
____

4. ____
____

5. ____
____

Date ______________

1. ____
____

2. ____
____

3. ____
____

4. ____
____

5. ____
____

I am **grateful** for...

Date _______________

1. ____
____

2. ____
____

3. ____
____

4. ____
____

5. ____
____

Date _______________

1. ____
____

2. ____
____

3. ____
____

4. ____
____

5. ____
____

I am **grateful** for...

Date ______________

1. ____
____

2. ____
____

3. ____
____

4. ____
____

5. ____
____

Date ______________

1. ____
____

2. ____
____

3. ____
____

4. ____
____

5. ____
____

I am **grateful** for...

Date ______________

1. ____
____

2. ____
____

3. ____
____

4. ____
____

5. ____
____

Date ______________

1. ____
____

2. ____
____

3. ____
____

4. ____
____

5. ____
____

I am **grateful** for...

Date ______________

1. ____
____

2. ____
____

3. ____
____

4. ____
____

5. ____
____

Date ______________

1. ____
____

2. ____
____

3. ____
____

4. ____
____

5. ____
____

I am **grateful** for...

Date ______________

1. ____
____

2. ____
____

3. ____
____

4. ____
____

5. ____
____

Date ______________

1. ____
____

2. ____
____

3. ____
____

4. ____
____

5. ____
____

I am **grateful** for...

Date ______________

1. ____
____

2. ____
____

3. ____
____

4. ____
____

5. ____
____

Date ______________

1. ____
____

2. ____
____

3. ____
____

4. ____
____

5. ____
____

I am **grateful** for...

Date ______________

1. ____
____

2. ____
____

3. ____
____

4. ____
____

5. ____
____

Date ______________

1. ____
____

2. ____
____

3. ____
____

4. ____
____

5. ____
____

I am **grateful** for...

Date ______________

1. ____
____

2. ____
____

3. ____
____

4. ____
____

5. ____
____

Date ______________

1. ____
____

2. ____
____

3. ____
____

4. ____
____

5. ____
____

I am **grateful** for...

Date ______________

1. ____
____

2. ____
____

3. ____
____

4. ____
____

5. ____
____

Date ______________

1. ____
____

2. ____
____

3. ____
____

4. ____
____

5. ____
____

I am **grateful** for...

Date ______________

1. ____
____

2. ____
____

3. ____
____

4. ____
____

5. ____
____

Date ______________

1. ____
____

2. ____
____

3. ____
____

4. ____
____

5. ____
____

I am **grateful** for...

Date _______________

1. ____
____

2. ____
____

3. ____
____

4. ____
____

5. ____
____

Date _______________

1. ____
____

2. ____
____

3. ____
____

4. ____
____

5. ____
____

I am **grateful** for...

Date ______________

1. ____
____

2. ____
____

3. ____
____

4. ____
____

5. ____
____

Date ______________

1. ____
____

2. ____
____

3. ____
____

4. ____
____

5. ____
____

I am **grateful** for...

Date ______________

1. ____
____

2. ____
____

3. ____
____

4. ____
____

5. ____
____

Date ______________

1. ____
____

2. ____
____

3. ____
____

4. ____
____

5. ____
____

I am **grateful** for...

Date ______________

1. ____
____

2. ____
____

3. ____
____

4. ____
____

5. ____
____

Date ______________

1. ____
____

2. ____
____

3. ____
____

4. ____
____

5. ____
____

I am **grateful** for...

Date _______________

1. ____
____

2. ____
____

3. ____
____

4. ____
____

5. ____
____

Date _______________

1. ____
____

2. ____
____

3. ____
____

4. ____
____

5. ____
____

I am **grateful** for...

Date ______________

1. ____
____

2. ____
____

3. ____
____

4. ____
____

5. ____
____

Date ______________

1. ____
____

2. ____
____

3. ____
____

4. ____
____

5. ____
____

I am **grateful** for...

Date ______________

1. ____
____

2. ____
____

3. ____
____

4. ____
____

5. ____
____

Date ______________

1. ____
____

2. ____
____

3. ____
____

4. ____
____

5. ____
____

I am **grateful** for...

Date ______________

1. ____
____

2. ____
____

3. ____
____

4. ____
____

5. ____
____

Date ______________

1. ____
____

2. ____
____

3. ____
____

4. ____
____

5. ____
____

I am **grateful** for...

Date ______________

1. ____
____

2. ____
____

3. ____
____

4. ____
____

5. ____
____

Date ______________

1. ____
____

2. ____
____

3. ____
____

4. ____
____

5. ____
____

I am **grateful** for...

Date ______________

1. ____
____

2. ____
____

3. ____
____

4. ____
____

5. ____
____

Date ______________

1. ____
____

2. ____
____

3. ____
____

4. ____
____

5. ____
____

I am **grateful** for...

Date ______________

1. ____
____

2. ____
____

3. ____
____

4. ____
____

5. ____
____

Date ______________

1. ____
____

2. ____
____

3. ____
____

4. ____
____

5. ____
____

I am **grateful** for...

Date _______________

1. ____
____

2. ____
____

3. ____
____

4. ____
____

5. ____
____

Date _______________

1. ____
____

2. ____
____

3. ____
____

4. ____
____

5. ____
____

I am **grateful** for...

Date ______________

1. ____
____

2. ____
____

3. ____
____

4. ____
____

5. ____
____

Date ______________

1. ____
____

2. ____
____

3. ____
____

4. ____
____

5. ____
____

I am **grateful** for...

Date ______________

1. ____
____

2. ____
____

3. ____
____

4. ____
____

5. ____
____

Date ______________

1. ____
____

2. ____
____

3. ____
____

4. ____
____

5. ____
____

I am **grateful** for...

Date ______________

1. ____
____

2. ____
____

3. ____
____

4. ____
____

5. ____
____

Date ______________

1. ____
____

2. ____
____

3. ____
____

4. ____
____

5. ____
____

I am **grateful** for...

Date _______________

1. ____
____

2. ____
____

3. ____
____

4. ____
____

5. ____
____

Date _______________

1. ____
____

2. ____
____

3. ____
____

4. ____
____

5. ____
____

I am **grateful** for...

Date ______________

1. ____
____

2. ____
____

3. ____
____

4. ____
____

5. ____
____

Date ______________

1. ____
____

2. ____
____

3. ____
____

4. ____
____

5. ____
____

I am **grateful** for...

Date ______________

1. ____
____

2. ____
____

3. ____
____

4. ____
____

5. ____
____

Date ______________

1. ____
____

2. ____
____

3. ____
____

4. ____
____

5. ____
____

I am **grateful** for...

Date ______________

1. ____
____

2. ____
____

3. ____
____

4. ____
____

5. ____
____

Date ______________

1. ____
____

2. ____
____

3. ____
____

4. ____
____

5. ____
____

I am **grateful** for...

Date ______________

1. ____

____

2. ____

____

3. ____

____

4. ____

____

5. ____

____

Date ______________

1. ____

____

2. ____

____

3. ____

____

4. ____

____

5. ____

____

I am **grateful** for...

Date ______________

1. ____
____

2. ____
____

3. ____
____

4. ____
____

5. ____
____

Date ______________

1. ____
____

2. ____
____

3. ____
____

4. ____
____

5. ____
____

I am **grateful** for...

Date ______________

1. ____
____

2. ____
____

3. ____
____

4. ____
____

5. ____
____

Date ______________

1. ____
____

2. ____
____

3. ____
____

4. ____
____

5. ____
____

The **Gratitude** Journal

About the Creators

Eric Dykstra is a former freaked-out Christian overachiever who is now resting in the grace of God found in the New Covenant. He and his wife Kelly founded The Crossing, a multi-site church north of Minneapolis. Eric's passions include seeing broken people far from God come to know the amazing grace of Jesus, fishing on the Rum River for smallmouth bass, and traveling with his family. ***Grace on Tap*** is Eric's first book, released in 2013. He also co-authored ***Unhooked & Untangled****: A Guide to Finding Freedom from your Vices, Addictions, and Bad Habits*. Both books are available on Amazon and Amazon Kindle

Kelly Dykstra loves helping people discover that a life of faith is simpler than you'd think. Raised in Alabama, Kelly is a southern girl at heart. She finds great delight in olives, Mexican food, Starbucks, traveling, great high heels, and going out to eat with Eric and her kiddos, Braden, Holland & Aidan. ***The People Mover*** is Kelly's first book, released in 2014. Available on Amazon and Amazon Kindle.

You can find Eric & Kelly's ministry and sermons on **freegrace.tv**.

The Crossing Church (freegrace.tv) is based in Elk River, Minnesota, with campuses in surrounding towns. It is known widely for its unique approach to reaching those who feel the need for God's grace the most. The grace message and its accompanying Holy Spirit power is continually transforming the people of The Crossing.

The Crossing College (TheCrossingCollege.com) equips members of the Body of Christ to live out their calling.

Crossing Creative (CrossingCreative.com) leads The Crossing Church in worship and publishes original worship music. ***Grace is Life*** is their debut album, combining intentional, grace-centric lyrics with their signature rock & roll-style of worship. Their second album is called ***Found My Worth***. Both are available on iTunes and Amazon.